Students Under Siege

Students Under Siege

The Real Reasons behind
America's Ongoing Mass Shootings
and How to Stop Them

Bud Harris, PhD

Daphne
Publications

DAPHNE PUBLICATIONS • ASHEVILLE, NORTH CAROLINA

STUDENTS UNDER SIEGE: THE REAL REASONS BEHIND AMERICA'S
ONGOING MASS SHOOTINGS AND HOW TO STOP THEM

COPYRIGHT © 2018 BY BUD HARRIS, PH.D.

DAPHNE PUBLICATIONS, AN IMPRINT OF SPES, INC.

Harris, Clifton T. Bud
Students under siege: the real reasons behind America's ongoing mass shootings and
how to stop them / Bud Harris

ISBN 978-0-578-43050-8   Non-Fiction
1. Violence in Society   2. Social Psychology

Cover Design: Courtney Tiberio
Interior Design: Susan L. Yost

FROM THE BRUTAL LOSS OF OUR CHILDREN and loved ones, let us show we will derive not confusion, more fear and weakness, but strength—the strength to face our reality and the courage to prove to our children we value them. Let the torment of these terrible events bind us together in a new fellowship—making us one people beginning a new chapter in our history.

CONTENTS

INTRODUCTION

This short work is a challenge to face the reality behind our shock and heartbreak, to understand the core of what is happening in our culture, and how to take a major step forward together in caring for each other.

Every child has the right to be safe in school. School murders, church murders, and other mass murders are one of the most important challenges facing us today. Together we will explore how our common pain should lead to a determined effort to understand the very core of these heartbreaking events, to come to a common purpose and then take action. We will explore the factors and failures that have manifested in the anxious desire to have military grade weapons on a massive scale.

Then this work will journey deep into the human, social, and psychological dimensions of how a mass murderer is formed.

I will do my best to help us trace the painful influences and failures that have brought us to this place of danger and heartbreak. Then as I write I will offer us the opportunity to accept the hard realities and challenges necessary to restructure our culture's value system into one where we care for each other and prove to our children we value them.

Because I have felt these outrages very personally and have been so inspired by the active response of the students of Marjory Stoneman Douglas High School, I am writing this small book as a letter to them. Throughout my writing, the lingering theme in the background is "Do we have the courage to face our failures and prove we value our children and each other?"

Dear Students,

There are no words to express our sense of shock and horror at the mass murders of your classmates. There are no words sad enough to express our sense of loss. These terrible events have thrust upon us our duty as parents, grandparents, and citizens of the United States to do away with the fear, the indifference, and the dehumanization that is infecting our society and show that we are capable of decisive action. There must be no words strong enough to express our determination to continue the forward thrust of the crusade you students have started.

The world is under fire, and we have been hiding under the bed.

GETTING OUT FROM UNDER THE BED

I thought I had said all I have to say about this topic after the shootings, the murders, in the church in Charleston, South Carolina. I thought I had said all I have to say in the blog I wrote at the time. But I was wrong. Since then we have had a presidential election, the world has changed, and we adults need to quit hiding under the bed. My inner muse who connects me with the voice of my soul compelled me to write another book, *America Now: Facing Fear and Division to Reclaim the Heart of Our Democracy*. During that process I realized I have a lot more to say about these types of murders—a lot more—and, as hard as it is for me to think about them, I have to get out from under the bed and say what I think.

There is no question about the fire that moves me now, which is the response of you students to seeing your friends murdered. In pain and rage you have refused to be victims and have become warriors and crusaders. You are showing us the best of our American tradition, which is the determination to stand up to any challenge no matter how daunting it is.

I am humbled as I have watched and listened to you. You have caused me to realize I must look in the mirror, into my own soul, and into my responsibility as an elder and a citizen in the history of these events. I know all too well that being under the bed, ignoring or denying the evil around me, is in fact a way of being engaged in it.

> *So I must say with deep regret that my generation has failed you. I have failed you. The generations we parented have failed you. We have failed to recognize the real problems behind these continuing murders.*

Our democracy has failed you. Our democracy has become weak because of our, the older generations', shallow approach to it and the large number of people who have given up on it. You saw the results of this failure by the lack of what happened when you encountered your state legislature and after you visited the president.

The first step in being able to learn from and grow beyond our failures is to recognize them, accept them, and confront them. Unless we have the humility and the courage to carry out this encounter, we will discover that our failures will repeat themselves continually. I believe that we can face our failures and awaken our hearts.

*   *   *   *

Too many people, like me, have thought it is enough to work hard, try to provide for our families, contribute to charities, and vote. Because of our blindness we have failed to see the intensity of the suffering around us that is dehumanizing so many of us—that is creating an atmosphere of stress, anxiety, fear, and violence. Focusing our lives too narrowly has kept us from facing the real problems in our society and from doing the right things to relieve them. Now it is time for us to step up to the plate with the determination to reform our government into the values it was created for: the sacredness of every person and liberty, equality, and opportunity for everyone. We can't afford to hate each other. We can't afford to elect officials who foster divisiveness, pander to our weaknesses, and inflame our fears and anger. We must be determined to assure our future generations that our diversities will be glued together by our active citizenship.

It is a challenge for you students, but I implore you to make your wounds from these murders sacred wounds.

Let them fuel the spiritual fire that never allows you to stop leading the way to change. Do not let yourselves fall into bitterness or despair. Yet do not heal your trauma. Do not try to adjust to or absorb your pain. We have been doing that for too many decades. We elders must also keep the murdered children alive in our collective memories and in our hearts. To keep a democracy alive, we have to learn that we must always be activists.

Keep your pain alive. Give it a special chamber, a sacred container in your heart where you can carry it—where it will be an eternal flame for your warrior spirit until we have made our world safe for every child.

I want to assure you that I am praying hard that we elders will become young at heart, step out of our comfort zones, and take the needed actions and risks to change our country into a safe one. I pray that we will bring our social awareness and our consciences out from under the bed. That we will make the commitments and welcome the challenges to make our country safe for our children and grandchildren. For our own self-respect, we in the older generations must join you wholeheartedly. We must realize that if God doesn't judge us, history will, and our grandchildren are being called to judge us right now.

*   *   *   *

We have one hell of a problem that we haven't confronted or even admitted we have. Most of us haven't even asked ourselves this most basic question:

Why do so many people insist they need to have military grade assault weapons to begin with? And why are they so terrified of losing them?

Now let me be clear before I address this question. Both I and the students in Parkland want to treat responsible gun owners with respect. We must stop the name calling, polarization, and self-righteousness on all sides. All of us need to do some soul searching and we need the help of responsible gun-owners—we all need to help stop these tragedies and begin a new chapter in our history. We aren't advocating taking away guns used for self-protection, sport shooting, or hunting. Nor do we mean guns that are handed down in families, as they were in mine. Nor are we suggesting negating the second amendment or advocating for sending stormtroopers into respectable homes. These scenarios are impossible as well as ludicrous under our laws. When we hear these kinds of threats, we should understand that they actually are lies told by politicians, certain parts of the media, and special-interest groups. These lies are meant to scare us into thinking that if we lose our guns we will lose our liberty and our right to justice leading us to be crushed by instant tyranny. These lies are meant to scare us into voting for particular candidates and supporting special-interest groups.

So to rephrase, the real question we need to ask is:

Why do so many of us want to own weapons designed to kill human beings, weapons designed for mass murder? What is it that makes us terrified of losing those weapons?

IS IT ABOUT THE FEAR I DON'T MATTER?

In order to set the stage for answering this question, I want to share two stories with you from my clinical background as a Jungian psychoanalyst.

The first one was told to me by Michael, who was a middle-aged physician. He felt stuck, frustrated, and hopeless in his job. Four years previously, Michael had moved with his family to a lovely small mountain town close to where I live in Asheville, North Carolina, to get away from congested city life. He took a job as an internist in a clinic owned by a regional hospital and medical center. This group had been buying up practices and clinics throughout the area. Michael's wife had made friends and loved the area. His children were doing well in the local high school. Michael, however, had been on antidepressants for the last two years and was beginning to hate his job.

During lunch one day, he confided in Fred, a fellow physician in the practice, about how trapped he was feeling. As they talked, Michael said he had become a physician in order to be a healer, a people person. Now, he told Fred, he felt like an assembly line worker. Every year when his contract was renewed, his quota of patients to be seen, which determined his pay and whether he could keep his job, went up. In addition, his requirements for keeping medical notes, coding, entering treatment plans and prescriptions, and so forth got more complicated. He told Fred that to keep his pay from dropping he spent most of his time with a patient facing his computer and had little chance of developing a real rapport with the actual person. He believed this robbed his patients of the best care and robbed him of the possible satisfaction in his work. Michael also felt trapped because his contract had a noncompete clause in it covering a radius of one hundred miles. This clause meant that if he left his job he would have to jerk his family out of their community and school in order to move somewhere else.

Fred responded that he felt exactly the same way and invited Michael out to his place in the country Saturday afternoon to talk more about their dilemma. When Michael arrived, Fred ushered him into his den for a beer and to talk. Michael told me, "When I walked into his den, I thought I was in the armory at a military base. Of course, everything was safely locked down." As the afternoon wore on, Fred invited Michael to step out back and do some shooting into the bank of dirt behind the house. Michael said to me, "I'd never fired a gun in my life. But Fred was very careful in showing me how to use and handle the guns safely. We fired for about twenty minutes, on semiautomatic and automatic. Damn! I was surprised. As soon as I started, I felt a rush of adrenalin. I felt the power. Later as I was driving home, I realized I had felt a sense of power firing it—and I didn't feel depressed." Michael paused and then said, "These thoughts are absolutely scary to me. Fred told me shooting is his therapy. That thought scares the hell out of me, too."

After his second shooting experience with Fred, Michael said he woke up in the middle of the night and rage was boiling out of him. "God!" he said, "No wonder I'm depressed. I must have repressed this for years. How in the hell has my once honored profession, that I thought was going to be a sacred calling, become reduced to piece work? Where is the purpose and dignity I expected?" Far too many of us—blue-collar workers, white-collar workers, specialists, and professionals—are asking why our desire for work that makes a contribution and provides a decent life has been reduced to a pressured, meaningless, insecure activity. I, for one, don't believe we can afford to accept this state of affairs that is so disturbing.

*   *   *   *

My second story is about Marlene, an attorney with two young children. They live in an upper-middle-class area in our medium-sized town. Her husband had recently blindsided her by leaving the family. Marlene felt betrayed and vulnerable. There had also been several break-ins in her neighborhood which increased her feelings of vulnerability. Marlene decided to get a license to have and carry a handgun. She first took her gun to a local firing range to get instructions about gun safety and training in firing it. She told me, "As soon as I started firing it, I felt a rush. I felt powerful. I still go to the range once or twice a month. I love having this sense of power."

*   *   *   *

Neither Michael nor Marlene has any desire to own a gun designed for the mass destruction of human beings. So what do their stories have to do with my question of why so many of us want to own weapons of mass destruction and why we are so afraid of losing them? Just this. We have been living in a rising sea of stress, anxiety, and fear for decades. Toxic stress comes from anxiety and fear. Anxiety is caused by threats or perceived threats that are beyond our control. Fear comes from the anticipation of or the appearance of things or situations that threaten us directly. Threats may be physical, emotional, psychological, or all of the above. I wonder if, through repression and denial and the illusions of positive thinking that things are always getting better, we have become adjusted to living with toxic stress, anxiety, and fear. I wonder if we no longer realize how prevalent they are and how much they dehumanize us. Have we become like fish who aren't aware they are swimming in a very polluted ocean?

At a subliminal level we must know we are living in a society where we are feeling increasingly threatened and powerless.

The reality is we don't feel safe. Our jobs do not feel secure. Our streets don't feel safe. Medical costs can wipe us out. College costs can bury us and our children for decades. Getting a decent job at any age, at any level, has become a challenging, humiliating experience.

And the list goes on. In addition, as you students in Parkland have discovered, we don't feel like we have any power in our democracy. Nor, in general, do we feel like our government on any level gives a damn about our welfare.

Could it be that this demand for assault weapons in our society is trying to teach us how much we fear the ruthlessness that dominates our world? Doesn't the NRA offer a community for people who are afraid and want a solution? Don't too many of us want and feel the need for a gun simply because deep inside of ourselves we want to have a personal sense of empowerment as a human being?

*   *   *   *

This path of thinking led me to wonder why people in other developed nations aren't as frantic to have killing machines as we are. Of course, I also wondered why they are not shooting each other at anywhere near the same rate as we are. Well, I've lived for a number of years in some of these countries, and while they have their problems, their citizens simply feel a lot more secure than we do. I believe there are several reasons they feel more secure.

To begin with, they have better job security. Their jobs can't be jerked out from under them. When industries change, the transitions are managed and they have comprehensive safety nets. In general, the countries respect their citizens' right to be able to enjoy the rewards of hard work, have faith in the future, and keep their communities intact.

In addition, these countries have healthcare for everyone for life. And no matter what you have heard from politicians and vested interest groups, their systems are better on the average than ours, which is by far the most expensive in the world. The last time I looked at the World Health Organization's statistics, we were ranked thirty-seventh, just ahead of Cuba.

Then, these countries have free university training. Young adults and their families are not saddled with huge educational debts for decades.

Moreover, they have a livable minimum wage. People who work can hope for a decent life.

They also have respectable retirement benefits. Good retirement benefits and medical care help everyone face the future without dread.

Plus, and what really stuns me, they are more democratic than we are. In general, wealth and political influence are much more separated than in this country. Campaigns are short and stop a few days before elections to give citizens time to think and make their decisions.

I would also like to point out that these developed nations are not, in fact, socialist. They all have free-market capitalist economic systems.

IT'S DARK UNDER THE BED

Listen up, students at Parkland. You are on the right track. Get out the vote! Change needs to be deeper than we let ourselves think. I am staggered when I look at other developed countries and how they support their citizens. I believe we have been sold a pack of very destructive lies that such support here would impose gigantic tax burdens and hinder individual freedoms. We don't consider how much money these benefits would save in other social costs such as law enforcement, prisons, medical costs, and reducing the high costs of addiction, depression, and anxiety, which are epidemic in our society. Nor do we consider how these benefits would save our corporations and businesses money, making more small businesses possible and making our large ones more competitive in the world market.

But here's the biggest thing we ignore, what all of our anxieties and fears add up to. I believe so many of us want our guns in the hope that they can give us power over the fears, often the desperate fears, and even the desolation that we are hiding in our hearts, afraid to admit to ourselves.

Too many of us are afraid of losing our jobs, of being diminished in them, of losing our community and our place in it, of feeling humiliated and helpless or actually disgraced, of losing our savings, of becoming impoverished, of losing hopes and dreams or being robbed of the capacity to have them, of being victims of crime—and most of all, of being dehumanized and stripped of personal worth and power in the general pool of our society.

* * * *

You students in Parkland, and I hope many are joining you, must keep demanding for this to become a turning point in our history. This is a time we must seek to understand the sources of our fears, our polarizations, and the ways we are dehumanizing each other. We must examine how we have created a culture that is diminishing and alienating so many of us—especially our young people. Facing the cause of our frightening reality and speaking the truth to ourselves can give us the ability to reclaim our democracy and lead us into a new and revitalized future. Understanding these mass shootings must start with this step.

IS IT ABOUT THE FEAR I DON'T MATTER?

So, the second question we need to ask ourselves is:

Why do some of us end up being mass murderers?

In this question I am speaking about out-front mass murderers, especially those in schools; I am not speaking about the secretive killers who hide their victims' bodies and sometimes murder people one person at a time for years. So let's take a look at the history of school shootings. Justin Gruber from Parkland said at the White House, "I am only fifteen years old. I am a sophomore. Nineteen years ago, the first school shooting, Columbine, at Columbine High School, happened. And I was born into a world where I never got to experience safety and peace." Yes, Justin, but I am ashamed to say the first school shooting was not nineteen years ago. It was fifty-two years ago at the University of Texas Tower in Austin, Texas. Fourteen people were killed and thirty-one wounded by one shooter using semiautomatic weapons.

This dramatic tragedy compelled two of our greatest psychological thinkers and social commentators, Erich Fromm, PhD, and Rollo May, PhD, to extensively study and explain what was taking place in our society to produce such a staggering catastrophe. This is a crucial question.

What is taking place in our *society* to produce such a staggering catastrophe? Not what is taking place in this *person*.

Both men, as experienced psychoanalysts, knew these types of events are not the result of some kind of simple mental breakdown. In their great books *The Anatomy of Human Destructiveness* and *Power and Innocence: A Search for the Source of Violence*, these two great thinkers came up with the answers. Unfortunately we have been hiding under the bed—we have been too busy, too blind, too far into self-interest—and simply put, too weak to face the answers we need to face. Because of our failure we have remained victims.

> *Thank you, students in Parkland, for becoming warriors for the soul of our culture. Don't ever stop! And I will repeat: I am urging everyone in my generation and the ones we raised to come out from under the bed and join you.*

Dr. Fromm and Dr. May both came to the clear conclusion that if we are dehumanized to the point of feeling totally alienated from ourselves, our emotions, our potential, and our ability to belong to and function in our social tribe, we become destructively evil. Alienation—the extreme, isolated, and hopeless state of dehumanization, of feeling invisible even to one's self—causes a profound inner rage. It can result in the urge—or the compulsion—to destroy life, social structures, and even self. Alienated individuals can become trolls on the internet, and if they are cut off far enough from themselves and society, they can become murderers and serial rapists. Dr. Fromm called these life destroying actions malignant aggression. When alienated people come together they become militia groups, cults, and terrorists. Alienated citizens can also vote against their own self-interest out of rage and despair.

Nikolas Cruz in Parkland, like most of these murderers, wanted to wreak destruction and gain huge publicity by destroying in order to symbolically scream, "I exist! And this is my revenge for being denied that." Like other shooters, he finds his identity in resentment, rage and his ability to destroy life.

The first step in solving any problem is to recognize it. This means we must have the courage—let me repeat that—the *courage* to face the true source of these murders and penetrate into the heart of darkness behind them. Then we must act. We must be willing to be strongly aggressive and determined in the service of live. This leads me to my third question.

CAN WE AFFORD NOT TO CARE FOR EACH OTHER?

One tearful parent cried out after the shootings at Parkland that those murdered students are "children of God." At this point I need to take a time out and scream myself. I am so angry that my words are inadequate—angry at myself, angry at my culture, angry at our ongoing ability to miss the point of these tragedies and what has been happening tragically to our society for over five decades. We have an amazing capacity for failing to seek the real causes of these horrible events. Instead, we try to focus on managing the symptoms. Then we tend to respond to these symptoms with our pet theories or by taking off on our favorite political tangents or solutions for the symptoms without seriously searching for the roots of what appears to be senseless violence. We need to listen to our children and grandchildren and make our society safe for them from the ground up.

Let us not overlook that arming teachers, increasing guards, and installing metal detectors are measures that may in fact add more rewarding challenges for the alienated person who is striking out rather than solving the problem. If we miss this moment to pursue real change, our self-destruction is going to increase. Surely we don't think this situation is acceptable in our country.

WE HAVE ANOTHER SERIOUS PROBLEM, WE ARE AFRAID OF FACING REAL LIFE

It is incredible how deaf, dumb, and blind we are to nonphysical pain. If you break a leg, have cancer, the flu, or some other disease, people sympathize and want to help you. They show you respect. If you are in an area where a hurricane has trashed everything, people rush in with boats, food, shelter, and all sorts of help. But if you are paralyzed with despair, scared to get out of bed, can't see a reason for living, have lost hope, or are just sinking into a swamp of bitterness and misery, it almost seems like no one can help you—or in fact really wants to try to help you. Plus, our addiction to positive thinking enables our denial of the psychological suffering around us, as well as our view of it as a personal, embarrassing, and humiliating failure.

In 1989, when my wife and I arrived in Asheville, North Carolina, we found a very active state mental health system. The offices in Asheville were welcoming and well staffed by psychiatrists, psychologists, social workers, and supporting staff. Counseling and therapy were available for adults, couples, families, adolescents, and children on a sliding scale depending upon income. This system was supported by two private psychiatric hospitals in the city, two solid addiction treatment programs, and a supporting network of private practitioners. My wife and I were glad to join this climate of professionalism and caring.

By the year 2000, all these facilities were gone—the state facilities, the psychiatric hospitals, the addiction treatment programs, and many of the supporting professionals. What happened to these programs fills me with a cold rage—a rage that eliminates my detachment and any chance of forgiveness. Where did they go, you might wonder? The answer is that "managed care" came on the scene. Under the rubric of cutting medical costs and delivering "better care," the true focus was on increasing profits.

Too many people have bought the illusion that therapy or counseling shows weakness and that all it consists of is vomiting one's feelings.

These are very destructive fictions. These former facilities had the purpose of helping people to build a foundation for living productively and responsibly, to build skills to break out of loneliness—which our research shows kills us. Our mental health systems were meant to help us find hope, direction, and the capacity to love, and to make a contribution to society. They were meant to express our caring for each other and our compassion for the truly mentally ill so they could live in dignity and their families could live securely.

The reality was this. If some man or woman was drowning in despair, anger, or confusion, if some teenage boy or girl was struggling to stay afloat, if some couple or family was caught in the riptides of modern life, if someone was caught in a hurricane of addictions, there was a safe harbor—a place to find care and support. Such a harbor gives support to the whole community. It gives parents, teachers, ministers, and even the police a feeling of security that facilitates empathy, caring for each other, and civility. It does so because we know our backs are covered if we pay attention, listen to each other, and get involved.

In a recent book, *Insane: America's Criminal Treatment of Mental Illness,* the author Alisa Roth points out that more than half the prisoners incarcerated in America suffer from some kind of mental illness (*New York Times* 5/27/18, p.11, BR). One study reports that 75 percent of all women in jail are mentally ill.

For God's sake, this isn't rocket science. We have a clear need for community mental health systems, hospitals, therapeutic communities, farmsteads, and recovery campus settings. We need to look in the mirror and ask ourselves: Are we becoming as blind to what's happening to some of our fellow citizens as the Germans were in the 1930s? We are treating each other in incredibly cruel ways. Surely we can't think this is acceptable in our country, the richest country in the world.

Take it from me—I know—I am a mental health expert. I have been in practice for over forty years. The fact that some of these shooters have seen several counselors or therapists does not mean that we have a mental health system or that these people couldn't have been helped. I did an internship on an inpatient adolescent unit in a state hospital in 1974. That unit did a good job of combining healing therapy with structured learning theory to help adolescents find themselves and the skills they needed for living responsibly. That institution, which was also a teaching hospital for Emory University, is now gone and nothing has replaced it, that is, except a new and bigger jail.

In my heart I know that the children who were murdered are children of God. The students who were traumatized are children of God, and in my heart I know the shooter in Parkland, Nicolas Cruz, is also a child of God. We have failed them all.

In the dark early hours after midnight, when I am lying awake, I have to ask myself: How can we spend over $68 billion on an endless war and can't support the needs of hearts breaking all around us?

We can do better than this, and once we have the courage to open our eyes, we are morally bound to.

YOU STUDENTS ARE SHOWING US COURAGE AND LOVE

You students in Parkland are showing us our failures, the hollowness and indifference of our politicians—whom we have allowed to flourish. You are showing us, the adults, that we need to change our values. And our politicians are proving another basic fact to us. There will be no meaningful gun controls, none of the benefits I've mentioned to give us safety, no real efforts to reduce our fear of each other and join us together as a national community, until we separate wealth and large corporate influences from our politics. Until we have meaningful campaign finance reform, we can forget about our government seriously considering any of us as sacred, or of liberty, equality, and opportunity as real values. You young adults from Parkland are right. We must act and we must vote, and the fight against vested interests that currently dominate our government will be a long, hard one. Our challenge is not to become great again. It is to face our failures and become greater than we are today—greater in vision, greater in compassion, greater in love and respect for each other, for life, for the world we live in, and in concern for the safety of our children.

We face these questions: Are we tough enough to make these changes? Are we as tough as our founders were when in 1776 they began a war against the most powerful nation in the world? They were tough enough to risk their lives, losing more battles than they won. They were tough enough to fight for six and a half years, achieving a surprising victory for the values of the human heart. Can we work in every election for six and a half years and re-enliven the values our country was founded on? I am reminded of Robert F. Kennedy's challenge to us during his great speech on humanity when he said, "We must do this, not because it is economically advantageous, although it is; not because the laws of God command it, although they do…we must do it for the single and fundamental reason that it is the right thing to do."

I need to do it because I love this country. I must do it because I love my children and my grandchildren. And I love your awakening us to this sacred quest, and I am with you every step of the way.

Sincerely,
Bud Harris, PhD

QUESTIONS FOR REFLECTION AND DISCUSSION

1. Do we have the courage to face our failures and prove we value our children?

    This is a key question for all of us to ask ourselves and each other.

    Do you have the courage to face your failures and prove you value our children?

    How have we failed our children? In what ways have we shown we do not value our children? What does this courage look like?

    List just a few ways of showing courage to face our failures.

    List a few ways of showing we value our children.

    How might you start today to show your courage and prove you value our children?

    What keeps you from doing these things, taking action?

2. Bud Harris writes of us adults hiding under the bed as we deny the reality or ignore the reality of evil happening in our world today. In what ways do you hide under the bed?

    What might it take for you to come out from under the bed? To face yourself? To be a responsible adult? Do you have the courage it takes to come out from under the bed?

In what ways will you know you have come out from under the bed?

3. Consider this question: Why do so many people insist they need to have military grade assault weapons to begin with? And why are they so terrified of losing them?

   Ponder this question for a while. What are military grade assault weapons? Why would an ordinary citizen want or need such a weapon? Are they used for sport shooting or hunting? What are they used for? What is under the fear of losing such weapons?

4. Now rephrase the real question: Why do so many of us want to own weapons designed to kill human beings, weapons designed for mass murder? What is it that makes us terrified of losing those weapons?

   We are no longer talking of weapons used in sport shooting or hunting animals, but weapons designed to kill human beings, sometimes in masses.

   Is there fear present in these situations? What are we afraid of? Where does this fear come from? Consider the fear "I don't matter."

5. Reread the stories of Michael and Marlene. Neither of these two ordinary people have a desire to own a gun designed for the mass destruction of human beings. But they are good examples of people living in a rising sea of stress, anxiety, and fear for decades. Toxic stress comes from anxiety and fear. We have become adjusted to living with toxic stress, anxiety, and fear.

What happens to us when we live for so long with toxic stress, anxiety and fear? What has happened to you? Take a deep breath as you reflect on the ways you are affected by toxic stress, anxiety and fear. Take a few minutes to list the ways your life has been affected.

What is the challenge for you to change this toxic way of living?

6. "Don't too many of us want and feel the need for a gun simply because deep inside of ourselves we want to have a personal sense of empowerment as a human being?" How would you answer this question? What does this question mean to you?

7. "Some of us want guns in the hope that they can give us power over the fears, often the desperate fears, and even the desolation that we are hiding in our hearts, afraid to admit to ourselves."

How does this statement resonate with you? What are some of your fears, hiding in your heart? Take several deep breaths as you allow some of these fears to come into the light, out of hiding. Courage is needed here. Take your time. Make a list. Reflect back to get a sense of how you may have changed. Why are bringing fears to light so important?

8. 52 years ago we experienced the first mass shooting of 14 people at the University of Texas Tower in Austin, Texas, by one shooter. Dr. Erich Fromm, and Dr. Rollo May, extensively studied what was taking place in our society to produce such a horrible event.

They asked what was taking place in our *society, not just in the shooter*.

Both men came to the conclusion that if we are dehumanized to the point of feeling alienated from self and others, we become destructive and filled with profound inner rage. Dehumanization, alienation and rage are happening in our collective society. What are your thoughts about dehumanization, alienation and rage taking place in our society today? Are you willing to discuss these powerful emotions and the effects with friends and family members? Is it easier to deny their existence? How can you accept the challenge to begin the conversation to bring these powerful forces to the light?

9. One parent at the school in Parkland cried that the students are children of God. What are your thoughts: are the murdered ones children of God, the traumatized ones children of God, and what of Nicolas Cruz, the shooter? Is he a child of God? Then what are all of us to do with the belief they are ALL children of God? Might this belief bring us out from under the bed?

10. Dr. Harris writes, "Keep your pain alive. Give it a special chamber, a sacred container in your heart where you can carry it—where it will be an eternal flame for your warrior spirit until we have made our world safe for every child."

How might you create such a container? Why is it necessary to keep pain alive? What are your thoughts of an eternal flame for your warrior spirit?

These words are a huge challenge for us. Are you able and willing to accept the challenge? How will you, as an individual, be changed by accepting this challenge?

11. How many of you own guns? How many have ever shot a gun…target practice, hunting, skeet shooting? Have you ever experienced the same or similar feelings of power described by Fred, Michael, Marlene after shooting a gun? Take a minute to reflect on those times. What was your state of being at the time? Overworked? Overwhelmed? Useless? Not good enough? Helpless and hopeless? Isolated? Alienated? What about feelings of fear?

All the above feelings mixed in with fear can be powerful motivators for taking action or acting out in some way. Every day, in our culture, finds us swimming in a murky sea of fear. Imagine the feeling of power that comes with firing a gun mixed with the feelings of fear. Can you imagine some relief coming to you as a result of firing a gun?

Recently, a friend in her seventies related this experience to me. She said, "I experienced firing a gun for the first time at a target practice range. My brother walked through the entire experience with me. I was only firing one shot at a time before it was time to pull the trigger again. One shot at a time was terrifying and powerful. Shooting a gun that fires repeatedly without stopping is scary and terrifying. And, at the same time, firing an automatic gun, which allows one to JUST shoot would give one a feeling of being very powerful. No thinking involved, or very little, I

31

can imagine this would give one a feeling of GREAT power."

So now, after reflecting, I find myself feeling compassion for those tired, worn out, overworked, isolated, alienated parts of myself. And, I now feel compassion for all those with similar feelings swimming in a sea of fear. We are not so different.

Spend some quality time with question 11. Reflect on times and situations where you may have felt similar feelings. How might we as a culture help those cope with anxiety, fear, isolation, alienation? How might we help by finding ways of feeling powerful that don't include guns? How might life in our country change?

The greatest challenge we face is to find ways to help those with strong feelings of isolation and alienation...to help ourselves and those individuals live together in compassion and love.

A NOTE OF THANKS

Whether you received this book as a gift, borrowed it from a friend, or purchased it yourself, we're glad you read it. We think that Bud Harris is a refreshing, challenging, and inspiring voice and we hope you will share this book and his thoughts with your family and friends. If you would like to learn more about Bud Harris, PhD and his work, please visit: www.budharris.com or www.facebook.com/BudHarrisPh.D/.

AUTHOR'S BIO

BUD HARRIS, PHD, as a Jungian analyst, writer and lecturer, has dedicated his life to helping people grow through their challenges and life situations into becoming "the best versions of themselves." Bud originally became a businessman in the corporate world and then owned his own business. Though very successful, he began to search for a new version of himself and life when, at age thirty-five, he became dissatisfied with his accomplishments in business and was challenged by serious illness in his family. At this point, Bud returned to graduate school to become a psychotherapist. After earning his Ph.D. in psychology and practicing as a psychotherapist and psychologist, he experienced the call to further his growth and become a Jungian analyst. He then moved to Zurich, Switzerland, where he trained for over five years and graduated from the C. G. Jung Institute. Bud is the author of fourteen informing and inspiring books. He writes and teaches with his wife, Jungian analyst, Massimilla Harris, Ph.D., and lectures widely. Bud and Massimilla both practice as Jungian analysts in Asheville, North Carolina. For more information about his practice and work, visit: www.budharris.com or www.facebook.com/BudHarrisPh.D.